Elvis Presley

CONTENTS

T0101502

HOW TO USE THE CD ACCOMPANIMENT:

THE CD IS PLAYABLE ON ANY CD PLAYER, AND IS ALSO ENHANCED SO MAC AND PC USERS CAN ADJUST THE RECORDING TO ANY TEMPO WITHOUT CHANGING THE PITCH.

A MELODY CUE APPEARS ON THE RIGHT CHANNEL ONLY. IF YOUR CD PLAYER HAS A BALANCE ADJUSTMENT, YOU CAN ADJUST THE VOLUME OF THE MELODY BY TURNING DOWN THE RIGHT CHANNEL.

ISBN 978-1-4234-6699-4

HAL•LEONARD®
CORPORATION
7777 W. BLUEMOUND RD. P.O. BOX 13819 MILWAUKEE, WI 53213

Visit Hal Leonard Online at
www.halleonard.com

◆1 ALL SHOOK UP

Words and Music by OTIS BLACKWELL
and ELVIS PRESLEY

VIOLA

② BLUE SUEDE SHOES

Words and Music by
CARL LEE PERKINS

VIOLA

Rock 'n' Roll Shuffle

❸ CAN'T HELP FALLING IN LOVE

VIOLA

Words and Music by GEORGE DAVID WEISS,
HUGO PERETTI and LUIGI CREATORE

◆4 DON'T BE CRUEL
(To a Heart That's True)

VIOLA

Words and Music by OTIS BLACKWELL
and ELVIS PRESLEY

⬥5 HOUND DOG

VIOLA

Words and Music by JERRY LEIBER
and MIKE STOLLER

❻ I WANT YOU, I NEED YOU, I LOVE YOU

VIOLA

Words and Music by MAURICE MYSELS
and IRA KOSLOFF

⬥7 IT'S NOW OR NEVER

Words and Music by AARON SCHROEDER
and WALLY GOLD

VIOLA

8 JAILHOUSE ROCK

VIOLA

Words and Music by JERRY LEIBER
and MIKE STOLLER

◆⑨ LOVE ME

VIOLA

Words and Music by JERRY LEIBER
and MIKE STOLLER

⓾ LOVE ME TENDER

VIOLA

Words and Music by ELVIS PRESLEY
and VERA MATSON

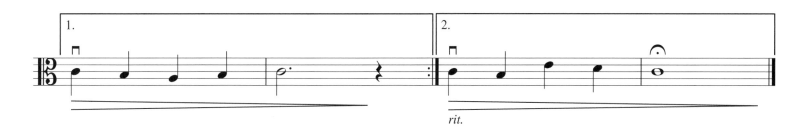

◆11 LOVING YOU

VIOLA

Words and Music by JERRY LEIBER
and MIKE STOLLER

RETURN TO SENDER

VIOLA

Words and Music by OTIS BLACKWELL
and WINFIELD SCOTT

13 (LET ME BE YOUR) TEDDY BEAR

VIOLA

Words and Music by KAL MANN
and BERNIE LOWE

◆14 TOO MUCH

VIOLA

Words and Music by LEE ROSENBERG
and BERNARD WEINMAN

◆15 WEAR MY RING AROUND YOUR NECK

VIOLA

Words and Music by BERT CARROLL
and RUSSELL MOODY